PREFACE

I've always been enthusiastic about hearing stories, and have maintained a positive opinion about them. I went through several challenges but always found a way to deal with it. With the world becoming ever fast and challenging it is very difficult for us to keep ourselves motivated.

So, here I present a few topics from your mundane life which may be helpful to keep pace with your current situation.

I want to make my sincere Thanks to my family members my dad, Mr. Stayendra Narayan Pathak, My mom Dr. Mamta Pandey and my friend and brother Abhigyan Swaroop.

It would be unjust to not mention Nimisha Banerjee for her all motivation and believing in me.

At last I want to thank Almighty for his graces.

For more details

Visit:www.mylifemotions.com

Follow Us on

Facebook, Instagram and Twitter

@mylifemotions

Contact us on

mylifemotions@gmail.com

START WHERE YOU ARE

"Start where you are,Use what you have"-Arthur Ashe

Have you ever wondered how many times you thought to start something new? Have you ever thought why didn't you start and worked upon a particular plan? And if you started it why did you give up soon after starting?

Can you find a common answer to this? Let me throw you a hint-You thought you didn't have enough resources or required talent.

In some shape or another, maybe, your answer was a match to it. Then there is something more you can ponder about, that is- every time you thought of starting a particular thing you knew you had something with you, maybe you had the talent but not resources or maybe resources but not all the talents required to execute it or maybe you had both but not the enough support from people around.

You may add a few more degrees to it, but you can never deny the fact that "you did have something".

Yes, this is the fact that all fingers of your hand are not equal, but then it is not expected from each finger to work alike. A cricket team is comprised of Batsman, wicket-keeper, all-rounder and bowlers. A batsman is expected to do according to his talent and the bowler is never expected to score a century or two.

A defender's job in soccer is to defend his goal post while striker is entitled to score a goal for team. The reason is simple we all have different talent and so we are to be evaluated accordingly,If defender focuses on his/her inability of not scoring a goal and Batsman give up playing because he doesn't know how to deliver a delivery will they be able to represent their team ever?

They concentrate on what they have and start to practice to sharpen their skills.

There are enough stories available to corroborate the fact that "Until you start with what you have You won't get what you want".

God has provided us with talents according to our abilities, So some of us are multitasking and multitalented while few of us are blessed with a single talent. So, it's our duty to find it and go with what we have got, there is no limit to which we can blame the world or The Almighty for what we don't have. At the end we are going to be evaluated on the basis of the fact -that's what talent we had and what justice we did with it.

Hence, start where you are and use what you have.

HOW TO CONCENTRATE ON SOMETHING COMPLETELY WITHOUT GETTING DISTRACTED?

So after you started you should have natural question as how to concentrate on it completely?

The resolution to this question lies in a book. It's 'Think and Grow Rich' by Napolian Hill.

You can get through this book, easily available in pdf format.

This book shows you the right path as how to induce faith in yourself and how to keep hold on what you have decided to do.

I will present you a gist of what is there in the book and how it will help you to ' concentrate on a particular thing without being distracted'

This book guides you through several laws and principles, my personal favorite is 'Auto suggestion'.

Let's help you out by telling main principles of this volume.

First Principle: Desire

For anyone to be successful, it is crucial that there exist within them the desire to be outstanding or at least better than their current state. Without this desire, there would be no motivation or cause for action. Simply wanting or a wish will not produce results as it is but wishful thinking. What is demanded is a deep burning desire for something that will automatically result in actions that will bring results. For true success, desire is necessary as wishes will only result in defeat. Desire focuses on the presence of something or the addition of something, whereas wanting focuses on the lack of something. Whenever you focus on the lacking part, you attract more lack into your life subconsciously. When you focus on the desire, you are consumed by the feeling of having that thing in your life to the extent that you are already picturing what it would feel like to experience it in your life. It is this desire that catapults you into action that brings consequences. Desire pushes you out of your comfort zone because when you desire something, you will not sit idly without doing everything possible to make the object of your desire. This creates the attraction and brings into your life everything you want.

Second Principle: Faith

When a desire stems and attracts emotions that arise from deep within one's belief, it attracts faith as well. For a desire to come true, you must have faith that it is possible and that it will come true. When you truly have faith in a desire and believe it will come true, it starts manifesting into its physical self. Those who believe they are not worthy of love, even on a subconscious level, often find themselves continuously in the same pattern of relationships that they somehow sabotage even if it may seem that they are the victims in it. This is because of our own deep existing beliefs.

Our beliefs hold so much power that they almost always come true so if you want a desire to become real, believe in it and have faith that it will come true. You have to truly believe that you deserve what you desire and it will be yours soon. It is faith that makes desires come true. If you find it is hard for you to have faith, repeat affirmations which state that the desire will come true. If you keep repeating something, it will start sounding true and soon enough the idea will not sound alien to you.

Monitor your beliefs and when you start identifying a pattern of self-limiting thoughts, pick deliberate affirmations and repeat them in order to counter the limiting beliefs.

Third Principle: Auto Suggestion

There is a strong reason why we do not believe in our own wishes and even though we want something, we do not believe we deserve it. This is a state of being brainwashed. We have been brainwashed by the society to believe we are unworthy of what we desire and that wanting something is sinful. Deep within us, these beliefs exist which makes it difficult for us to believe we deserve something.

In order to get rid of these beliefs, you need to meditate. Go somewhere quiet, relax your mind and repeat the beliefs you want to plant within you. Focus on your worthiness and having faith. With time, the seeds you plant during your meditative stage using affirmations will transform into beliefs. Additionally, start writing things you desire on small placards or notes and read them several times a day in order to remember what you want and place them firmly in your subconscious mind.

Fourth Principle: Specialized Knowledge

If acquiring knowledge ensured success, professors would be the wealthiest of the lot. However, that is as far from the truth as possible. Just having knowledge doesn't make one intelligent or even successful. This is proven by the fact that information is available to everyone these days. All the knowledge of the world is just a mere click away and yet few in the world are successful.

This is because it is not acquiring knowledge but using it that makes one successful. The correct use of specialized knowledge can make one successful which is why instead of focusing on gaining knowledge, focus on the knowledge that will make your desires come true and help you achieve success.

Fifth Principle: Imagination

Imagination can prove handy if used for the right purpose instead of just using it for one's entertainment. Creative imagination is the kind that comes in useful when you want to become successful. In other words, synthetic imagination is caused by the effects around us and creative imagination becomes the cause of the effects around us. When you use creative imagination to visualize and picture the fruits of your desires as a reality, they soon take form and in fact become a reality.

Sixth Principle: Organised Planning

In order to succeed, you need a concrete plan. This plan should be a way to achieve what you desire. Take your time to draft a plan and then write it down. Once you write it down, the chances of it becoming a reality increase, so always make sure that you write down your plans and then proceed to divide them into workable goals.

Seventh Principle: Decision

The type of decision Hill talks about in his book are firm and resolute decisions, instead of the ones that are formed and forgotten about in an instant. People who keep forming and changing their decisions are barely ever able to achieve what they desire. You need to believe strongly in your decisions to the extent that once you have taken a decision, it becomes concrete and must be followed through.

However, this it doesn't mean a decision cannot be changed. However, a decision that is changed regularly is not much of a decision. Take strong and well thought-out decisions and then see them through to the end.

Eighth Principle: Persistence

Many people fail at their first attempt. They might fail on their hundredth attempt but the simple fact is that the 100th failed attempt proves their dedication and this strength of desire will ensure they succeed at some point in the future. Many people give up on the first attempt, claiming that the challenge is too tough for them and as a result these people barely ever succeed. In order to succeed, there should be an unwavering quality to the desire. In other words, you want it and you will do anything and spend as long as it takes to make this desire a reality.

Ninth Principle: Power of the Master Mind

One of the most important principles, this principle explains that in order to achieve what you desire, you need to align your thought vibrations with similar vibrations which can be achieved by keeping company of like-minded people. By choosing your company wisely, you will be surrounded by the right kind of motivation that will inspire and challenge you. If, instead, you surround yourself with lazy people who tend to slack off, with time you will fall into the same mindset and forego all desires. By surrounding yourself with people who motivate you to reach higher, you will achieve more.

Tenth Principle: Transmutation

This is one of the more controversial points in Hill's book. He explains that we all have a strong sexual energy within us that we use to charm and attract the people we have an interest in. If we gather this energy and use it through creative imagination, we will be able to sound and seem more charming to people. This charm can help us get what we want by convincing people around us, through whom we may be able to achieve what we desire.

Eleventh Principle: The Subconscious Mind

Oftentimes, we truly want something but are limited by our beliefs and not being able to align vibrations in a manner that will help us make the desire a reality. We can control our subconscious mind by controlling and quieting our conscious mind and instilling the beliefs we want to see reflected in our lives. This is best achieved through meditation because we can truly control and tune into our subconscious. In simple words, our subconscious is the real master mind that decides what will and will not manifest in our lives.

Twelfth Principle: The Brain

According to research, when our creativity spikes, our subconscious mind reaches a state where it can be programmed comparatively easily which is why we need to be involved in creative tasks that help us get into the right state of the mind. When we repeat affirmations in our conscious mind while allowing ourselves to reach this state of mind through creative visualizations or imaginations, the pictures in our conscious mind are perceived as reality by our subconscious mind.

In simple words, when we visualize something, our subconscious mind cannot differentiate between the scene being a figment of our imagination or actual reality.

Final Principle: The Sixth Sense

This is your intuition or gut feeling and it becomes more profound when you start meditating and tuning into your subconscious mind. Your subconscious mind is your connection with the infinite wisdom of the universe. When we tune into our subconscious, which is in turn tuned into the universe, we get answers to our questions that would otherwise have eluded us. These answers may come to us as hunches or gut feelings and this is why they must not be ignored.

Hope, these principles help you to gain better concentration power

PROBLEMS-WHAT DO THEY SAY TO YOU?

So who likes problems?I guess none of us

But does our likes or dislikes really matter? I anticipate your response will be "NO" because you do know the problems are part and parcel of life

If you are living you ought to have some sorts of problems in animation.

To few problems are 'bugbear' which makes it unmanageable for them to live life peacefully. They don't know what to do and their mind goes into the turbulent state. **They desire to get rid of problems, but being in 'despondency'they hardly do a thing to drive them away.**

The consequence is obvious, they find themselves submerged in the ocean of depression.

In nut-shell seldom they take any action to overcome their agony and wait for a miracle, which all of us are cognizant of "Miracles are figments of our imagination".

Then here come charismatic people, full of spirit who take lessons from problems and always obtain a way to deal with them. They find a reason to be happy in whichever place they are and thus it acts as a source of "propulsion" for them.

They keep self belief and human action towards finding the root cause of problems at the same time keep themselves away from the blame game and finger pointing mode, because they know they have to rectify themselves not others.

So they lay every piece incoherent manner, the aftermath of which is problems recede gradually and revive them, making them even more courageous and enthusiastic about life.

Thus, choice is yours. I chose to be of second kind

PERFECTION-IS IT PERFECT?

It's perfectly normal that you are not perfect.

And if you claim that a person or thing is gross, I will just show you a mirror (which itself doesn't reflect light perfectly) and you will have the opportunity to see a dirty liar.

Some aren't well in sports while others are poor at studies, few can't sing good and some are not good at cooking, even Mr. Perfectionist doesn't have only Hit movies in his purse.

So, only perfect rule in this globe is that nothing is perfect.

Despite recognizing this fact, we curse our inabilities and do that one thing responsible for any hardships we suffer,

We only pay attention to a spot on white cloth instead of looking up to the beauty of the rest of the fabric.

The point here is we want everything to be perfectly perfect, reasons can be several for this avocation of ours.

Many of us aspire for perfection because we are afraid of being evaluated negatively if our work doesn't meet certain set standards.

Some of us take a run for perfection because we don't want to accept flaws in ourselves and obviously in whatever we do.

Another reason that can be adduced for the quest for perfection is, we are taught from our very childhood that society won't accept us if we aren't perfect.

But we forget one thing- Limit for attaining perfection is tending to Zero,it's never zero

So we just can't be utterly perfect.

Only thing One can do is update one's skills and not move for 100% perfection of particular skills that One already possess. There are several evidences to prove that only 20% of a person's skill is sufficient to extend out 80% of the task in hand, and it's also true that you can't take that task to 100% perfection with a rest of 80% of skill.

So, it's salutary to leave it right there

Even the app you enjoy most and use regularly, goes for updates sometime or other. The reason is simple and obvious, the earlier version wasn't perfect and nor will this be.

Any research paper always has a dedicated page for further extension,and now you the reason why.

Just think what would have happened if nature had dedicated good time of it in perfecting just one creation,would there have been so many creatures in this world?

Will any Company A survive in market that just produced only one perfect version?

or are there fair chances for Company B ruling market with updated version releasing over the span of years?

I suppose you will be in the right position now to decide the fate of these two companies in which one tried to be perfect while other tried to be updated.

Thus, it's good to breathe, slow down a little, let few things go, and concentrate on enjoying the journey because journey continues and perfection just halt your improvement since there won't be anything else to perfect about yourself.

POWER OF THE MASTER MIND

Every morning we wake and think to make the day better than previous ones, we do all we can, we essay to think differently, find way to do things in a way that it doesn't give monotonous results like everyday, we even try to not repeat what we ate yesterday.....

But why we do these things instead of following conventional plans which anyway will produce results,Why we challenge ourselves everyday in hope to achieve something new everyday?

The answer is obvious:

We all aspire to happiness, no matter what we do or what we think.... Our ultimate objective is to find happiness and be happier.

We all want to achieve serenity, satisfaction and joy, but are little unaware how to get them all. Hence, more often than not we find ourselves reading motivational quotes, watching something inspirational and at times attaching ourselves to people or things thinking this will change our way of life and will help to lead a life which is way more peaceful, full of satisfaction, joy and happiness.

But we forget that nature has granted us with powerful mind which can do all for us and help us to achieve what we want...

I will enjoin you a story which I read on the Internet today, just to achieve what you all want to achieve.... I.e. Something which motivates us and serve to achieve Happiness.

Here is the story in brief....

Long ago, there was an old man with his three sons in a deserted village, located in the vicinity of a desert. He had 17 camels, and they were the primary source of his income. He used to rent out camels as a means of embarking in the desert. One day, he passed away. He had left a will, leaving his assets for his three sons.

After the funeral and the other obligations were over, the three sons read the testament. While their father had split all the property he had into three equal parts, he had divided the 17 camels in a different way.

They were not apportioned equally among the three as '17' is an odd number and a prime number, which cannot be divided.

The old man had said that the eldest son will own half of the 17 camels, the middle one will get one third of the 17 camels, and the youngest one will get his share of camels as one ninth!

All of them were stunned to read the will and questioned each other how to divide the 17 camels as mentioned in the testament. It is not possible to divide 17 camels and pay half of the 17 camels to the eldest one. It is not possible also to divide the camels for the other two sons.

They passed several days thinking of ways to divide the camels as mentioned in the will, but none could find the answer.

They eventually took the issue to the wise man in their village. The wise man heard the problem and immediately found a solution. He demanded them to bring all the 17 camels to him.

The sons brought the camels to the wise man's home. The wise man added a camel owned by him and made the total number of camels 18.

Now, he asked the first son to read the testament. As per the will, the eldest son got half the camels, which now counted to 18 / 2 = 9 camels! The eldest one got 9 camels as his portion.

The remaining camels were 9.

The wise man asked the second son to read the testament. He was assigned 1 / 3 of the total camels.

It came to 18 / 3 = 6 camels. The second son got 6 camels as his part.

Total number of camels shared by the elder sons – 9 + 6 = 15 camels.

The third son read out his share of camels: 1 / 9th of the total number of camels – 18 / 9 = 2 camels.

The youngest one took 2 camels as his share.

Totally there were 9 + 6 + 2 camels shared by the brothers, which counted to 17 camels.

At present, the one camel aided by the wise man was taken back.

The wise man solved this problem smartly with his word.

Hmm... quite a mathematical story... but still you found easy to understand this one.. that's the power of your powerful brain

Coming to story and our situation....how does we relate?

Our entire life is like those 17 camels which we find hard to divide among different aspects of our life, until we mix our wisdom into it, the spiritual life is not lived and thus we can't achieve happiness, peace, satisfaction and joy.

LIFE WITHOUT REGRET

Most of us think of possibilities of **"if we had.."**

we all let ourselves get drowned in thoughts like **"i shouldn't .."** **"I regret doing.."** and list goes on and on.

We continue thinking and thinking, and hence seldom live a life we always wanted to live. We fail to notice what's going around us, start getting away from people we always loved and gradually we start living a life which is neither present nor in any way close to what wanted.

We develop a tendency of living two lives, one which we are actually living and another which we always aspired to... of course later one of our sub-conscious mind.

We easily grow a notion that we have wasted what we experienced, and what we have now is no where close to sufficient to achieve what I actually need. No wonder doing this creates our present miserable. This is start of infinite loop

i.e.

We again start regretting and blame ourselves in "our future's present" of not utilizing judiciously what we experienced then...

Finally, We doubt our potential and leave rest of life like a looser.....

Only antidote which can pull you out from this situation is YOU , your looking at things,and handling with situations one at a time and grabbing opportunities which are in front of you.

The past is passed and you did nothing wrong with it, Everyone takes the decision as per his/her assessment of that situation and so you shouldn't blame yourself that you took a wrong decision, Because you know you were right when the very situation was in front of you.